COHERENT

FRAGMENTS OF THOUGHT

PRIYANKA S. KUSHWAHA

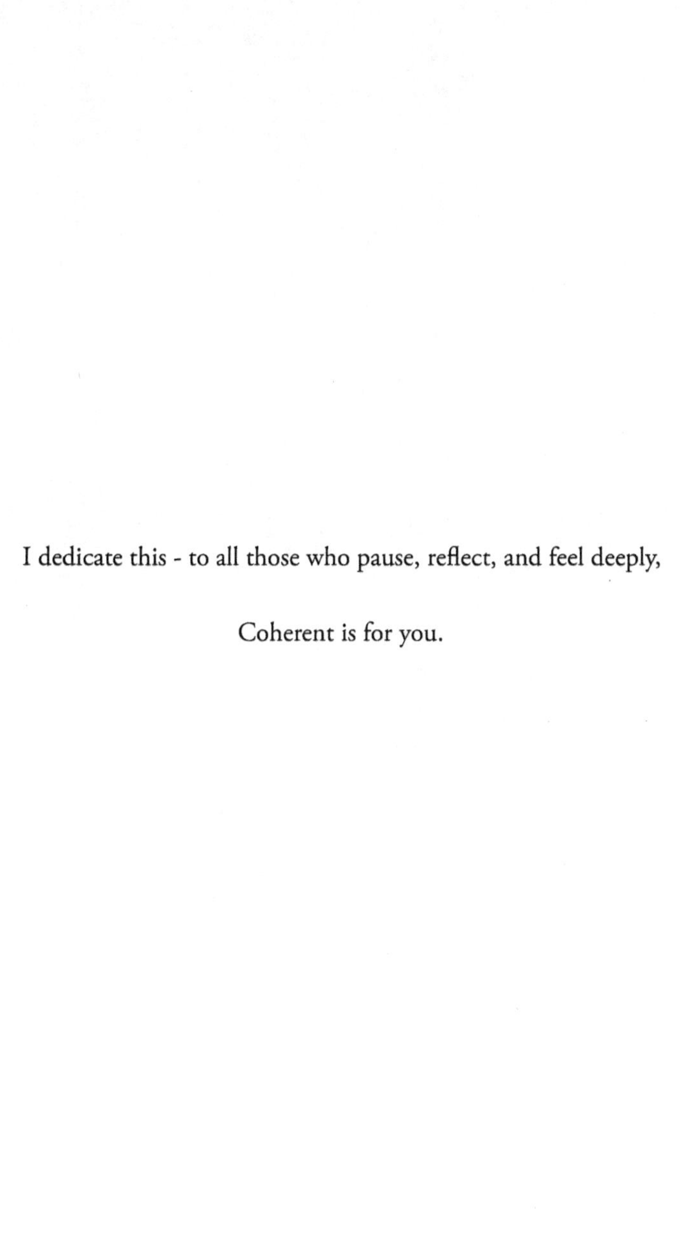

I dedicate this - to all those who pause, reflect, and feel deeply,

Coherent is for you.

Contents

Contents

Acknowledgements

This collection, Coherent, is not just a book; it's a reflection of the people and moments that have shaped me along the way.

First and foremost, I owe a deep and eternal gratitude to God, whose guidance, grace, and presence have been a constant source of strength throughout this journey. Without faith, none of this would have been possible.

To my mom and dad, your unwavering love and support have been my foundation. You believed in me even when I didn't believe in myself. Every step I take in this world is because of the sacrifices you've made and the love you've shown me. Thank you for being my strength, my safe haven, and my greatest inspiration.

To my husband, thank you for being the patient listener who has heard every line, every verse, and every pause. Your silent presence, always attentive and understanding, has been the quiet strength behind my writing. Your belief in my voice has given me the courage to share it with the world.

To my son, you have been my most honest listener, your curiosity and joy turning every day into a beautiful, unpredictable rhythm. Your innocence has taught me to hear the world in new ways, and for that, I am forever grateful.

I also owe everything to my family. You have been my steadfast anchors in the storm, believing in me when I faltered, supporting me when I needed strength, and cheering me on through every word. Your unconditional love has given me the courage to write and the confidence to share my heart.

To my friends, you are the quiet voices of encouragement and the loud echoes of joy that have made this journey worthwhile. Your belief in me, even in my moments of self-doubt, has been a gift I'll never take for granted. Thank you for understanding when I needed solitude to write and for being there when the words flowed freely.

A special thank you to Jijesh Nair for your brilliance and creativity in bringing Coherent to life with the cover design. Your work is a perfect visual companion to the words inside, and I'm beyond grateful for your artistic vision.

To my mentors and fellow writers who have shared their wisdom, challenged my perspective, and inspired me to keep going—you are the reason I've kept writing. Your guidance has shaped me not just as a poet but as a person.

Lastly, to the readers who embrace my words as their own. This book is yours as much as it is mine. Your connection to these poems breathes life into them and reminds me why I write.

And, of course, I would be remiss if I didn't thank the quiet moments of solitude—those spaces of stillness that allowed these poems to bloom. In silence, I found not just words but coherence.

Prologue

These poems are the resonance of my life — small echoes of moments I've lived, thoughts I've sat with, and feelings I've grown attached to over time. Some are born from things I've gone through personally, others from what I observe in the world around me — a passing glance, a quiet afternoon, a conversation that stayed with me longer than expected. I try to capture those everyday thoughts, the ones that slip in quietly but refuse to leave. Some of these pieces carry a lightness — playful, curious, simple. Others dip into heavier feelings, the kind that sit in the chest a little longer. And then there are those that ask questions — about life, about meaning, about what we're all doing here in the first place. There's no single theme, really, just a thread of honesty running through it all. This space is where I try to make sense of it, one poem at a time.

1. Coherent - selcouth lines

Ask me whether I would be the muse for someone one day?
My answer would be No!
I am not perfect to be the theory of someone's imagination.

Ask me whether I am artistic in my own way?
My answer would be No!
As I am still in a learning process of letting go.

Ask me whether my thoughts would stop someday?
My answer would be Yes! Maybe!
The day I die, my stories would die too,
but what will remain is my name
that I engrave in the coherent words of my selcouth lines.

2. My little boy

Tiny toes growing inch by inch,
With a grinning face, you look at me.
Your lips speak a thousand words; your endless stories make my world.
Your eyes are full of hope.
Your smile makes me stronger each day.
My little boy, you are my last love; without you, there is no better world.
The way you enquire about my day, no one made me feel special the way you do every day.
My loving boy, I know things will change and you will grow up soon, so let me hold you in my arms, until the time I reach those stars which might not be so soon.

3. Spoon and fork

It's a short love story of a spoon and a fork.

It bloomed and gloomed on the table top.

Lying next to the handful of plates together was how they always belonged.

Until one day, a butter knife took over the place. And cutting the edges with its dull face, it removed the spoon from its space.

The spoon decided to take its revenge and called his kins to show the knife its place.

But who would have known, the kins craved for something sweet and left the older spoon alone on the plate with a bowl of liquid soup.

4. House of Introverts

In solitude, we find peace.

In silence, we find ourselves.

The quiet clinks of glasses and plates,

Books are what we always crave

Getting lost in the woods is what we wish to navigate.

We stayed in a place full of crowd, yet we longed for stillness.

Now that we are here, this feels like home.

No shouting, no loud laughing.

A gentle nod and a knowing glance are enough to communicate.

Expressing through the writeups and poems .

This is what the House of Introverts looks like.

Each room is a sanctuary.

Each spot is a serene.

Echo of the sounds when we feel the will.

And the world that's roaring outside.

Time to think and time to explore the deep meaning of life.

Zen is the world we relate to.

Calmness and peace are the essence of each moment.

One step closer and two steps ahead is how we perceive our world.

This is what the House of Introverts looks like.

5. Date with self

I went on a date today with my younger self.
She looked a bit lost but had so much hope in her eyes.
I asked her how she was and how her days were going.
She couldn't stop talking—so full of excitement and dreams.
She trusted people so easily, her heart wide open.
I wanted to tell her that life isn't always as it seems,
that not everyone deserves her trust,
And that it's okay to slow down sometimes.
But I didn't. I just listened,
Letting her hold on to her innocence a little longer.
Then, she looked at me and asked how I was doing.
I told her I was okay, but that was only half the truth.
It wasn't that I was struggling—I just didn't have the words
anymore.

Over time, my innocence turned into desire,
And trust became complicated.
She wouldn't understand that yet.
I thought about letting her stay just the way she was,
Even though I wanted to protect her from all the pain ahead.
Life wasn't as easy as she believed.

But then, I saw my future self, sitting alone, lost in a book.
She looked up at me and shook her head, silently telling me,
"Don't do it."
I realized then that some lessons are meant to be learned, not
prevented.

6. I won't promise!

The key to my heart isn't easy to find,
but you are an exception.
I won't promise you the moon or a song—
They were never mine to give.
I won't swear to walk endless miles,
for life is uncertain, and death is inevitable.
I share my laughter with everyone,
but my sadness is mine alone to bear.
You are too special to carry that weight.
I'm done with love stories,
they no longer feel like mine.
I won't promise you the stars—
They belong to the sky,
and reaching them is far beyond my grasp.
So, I give you what is truly mine—
the key to my heart—
because you deserve to be there.

7. Change

Perfect to imperfect. Sane to insane.
Light to heavy and all vice versa.
Life isn't what it seems.
One day, we played with dolls and cars; the next,
we were entangled in jobs, bars, and wars.
Tell me, why did we change?
Tell me, why is nothing the same?
Genuineness lingers only in stories,
Chivalry now a relic of old glories.
Change—the only constant,
evitable, inevitable, relentless.

8. A foreigner within

As I moved to a place unknown,
I never knew how much I'd grow.
Truth was out, and so were faces,
Wishes were made, but prayers and fate had their places.
Distance brought some closer, yet pushed some away,
Lovers turned to foes, and foes chose to stay.
Life taught me lessons, one by one,
Things I once feared, I've now overcome.
Before this, I never put myself first,
Always giving, never knowing my worth.
But now, after all I've been through,
Going back is not what I'd do.
This life is mine, and I stand tall,
A foreigner within, yet I have it all.
Home is a memory, but I've come to see,
The real home I need is inside of me.

9. Time traveller

Sometimes, I feel like a time traveller,
drifting between the shadows of yesterday,
and the possibilities of tomorrow.
The past holds me captive,
its memories replaying like an old film,
making me wonder if I ever truly left.
Then, with a single thought,
I propel myself forward,
weaving dreams of a future yet to unfold.
In one breath, I am present;
in the next, I am lost—wandering through time,
hitched to what was, reaching for what could be,
yet never quite standing still.

10. End of winter

Each tradition has its own,
A fire is lit, and along comes the new dawn.
A fresh start with a golden hue,
Green leaves sprouting, smiles long due.
Yellow daffodils, red tulips bright,
Blossoms waking, chasing away the night.
My heart wonders at nature's grace,
Sadness fades, and joy takes its place.
Some play with colors, some dance with fire,
Celebrating life with endless desire.
This is how creation calls,
A cycle of seasons, a story for all.

11. Geometrical love

Let's align two lines,
forming an angle—
one perspective be yours,
the other is mine.
One shoots upward,
reaching beyond,
the other extends right,
steady and strong.
A single dot binds them,
the origin of all possibilities in time.
Now, let's draw another—
an obtuse line,
leaning back, yet holding firm.
This is where my love fits best—
falling, yet unwavering,
resting in its destined place forever.

12. A promise to myself

13. Poet in disguise

I picked up a canvas, ready to create,
But with no brush in hand, only a pen to relate.
I closed my eyes, letting my thoughts take flight,
Yet words, not images, filled my sight.

Lost and confused, I wept through the night,
Until it struck me—I might be a poet in disguise.
From that moment, I never cursed my gift,
But nurtured it with care, letting it grow and uplift.

14. Reflection

Looking at my reflection.

These fine lines on my neck and face,

Is this my age or just years of experience?

A painting worth hanging on a wall or a painting to hide from

them all?

Who am I? I asked my reflection.

It was quiet like a black and white figurine.

So then I wondered if I should ask an artist to paint me colorful.

Will he choose to even paint me?

Or will he be looking for another muse because I don't fit his

imagination?

15. Books half-read

Pages bookmarked, books half read
She picks up every new book, then puts it back on the shelves.
Only to start with another set and leave it half read..
Just like the unfinished chapters of her life,
she turned to new stories every now and then.

She called herself a book lover. But some called her fake,
some called her non-enthusiast,
and still she continued to hop from one story to another.

She knew what she was doing; the stack of unfinished books,
and the shamefulness that came along was part of her life now.
Yet every new chapter was close to her heart, and with every
little detail,
she embraced them a lot.
The weight of others' opinions tried pulling her into the darkness,
yet the light in her heart kept her hopes alive.

16. Waiting for you

There were no confessions,
No commitments,
Yet still I wait for you.
There were no promises,
No sacrifices,
Yet still I long for you.
You told me things ain't easy,
and you will be gone for some time now.
And all I could do was to reply to you in acceptance of things,
and not question you with how and why?

I don't know if you will be back.
I don't know if I will see you again.
The sound of your melodious voice.
The touch of your magical hands.
I still remember the car seat where it all bloomed once during
the rain.
I wrote a few letters and tore down the pages.
Yet again, I started writing only to crumble it into pieces and
put down the pen.
No calls, no messages, and I still keep you in my prayers.
I know you are not mine and will never be mine.
But I wish you happiness.
That is how my love for you will ever be defined.

17. Express yourself

Why be shy when they truly mean it?
Accept it as yours to keep.
You are beautiful in your own way—don't wait for others to say
it.
A simple smile, expressive eyes,
a face that glows even after a tearful night.
Your strength is your beauty.
Your struggle is beyond any words.
Yet, in a world that often forgets to appreciate,
compliments so rare are meant to stay when they are enunciated.
So, weave your thoughts into words,
and let them flow like a gentle stream.
Tell them their laughter paints the canvas,
their strength is like that untold poetry,
and their beauty radiates the light that is so hard to find.
Words can heal. They can embrace.
So, let them know—
These lines are theirs and forever to keep.

18. Rising through

They say the older you get,
the wiser you become, so,
Today, I let you go—
along with the echoes of your memories.
Today, I set my soul aflame,
not to consume myself in its fire,
But to burn up this lingering desire for you.
Today, I rise a step closer to my own light.
Call it ego if you must;
To me, it's self-respect.
Because I am done trying,
Done being the only one holding us together.
Today, I choose to look ahead,
embracing the promise of new experiences life has to offer.
Today, I immerse myself fully,
ready to explore the unknown and grow with every moment.

19. Unwanted Ego

Time flies, and people change.
What remains are memories clouded by unnecessary ego.
What if, that day, we had just talked?
What if we had greeted each other like any other day?
Torn between ego and love, life passed us by.
Then one day, everything changed,
and all we had left were memories,
and the loss caused by our pride.
Who really wins in the end—you or them?
Or is it that both lose?
A long-forgotten promise,
once the foundation of our bond,
is now just a shadow of what could have been.

20. Not just another day

Today is not just another day.
It's a day for celebration.
Not for you, but for me, it is, and for my family members.
As I cross another year,
I looked behind and saw myself.
What a journey! I must say.
With so many ups and downs on the way.
I sit here with a little pocket book in my hands.
Ready to write another chapter of another year.
I never thought that I would be one day.
And look here.
I am here to this day,
Crying and laughing and ranting all the way.

21. 40's

Nearing my 40s, and I color myself in red.

With few friends, and mostly the ones who talk behind my back.

With age comes what we call maturity,

And along comes her friends' humiliation, judgment, and a kind of parity.

Other people try to cheer themselves up with the era of instant reels.

And I am here, sulking about what I have not achieved.

I still pretend to be in my 20s, trying to learn new things.

Only to lose focus and then return to where I began,

looping in like an invisible ring.

22. Forgotten memories

Standing at the edge of forties
I undo the forgotten memories of my youth.
Youth, which I still try to find within me.
But all I found was the experience that comes with maturity.
Maturity is what I wanted to perceive during my twenties.
Now I wish to go back and repeat those mistakes,
how much they were filled with stupidity.
Stupidity, which I thought would definitely end one day,
caught me still in a fire while trying to hold on to the memories
that serve me no purpose,
however much I desire.
Desire the world, you said, and forty is the new thirty,
I keep saying to myself. Forgotten memories now reside inside
me,
but when I try to remember,
all it reminds me of is my grey hair slowly gathering above my
wrinkled eyes and cheeks.

23. Liar in disguise

Crafting a lie,
To make a beautiful sculpture.
But how long the sculpture would stand,
When inch by inch and at every step,
all were carved with lies.
The sculpture slowly begins to rot,
with all the perishable lies.
Bronze, marble, gold, and stone -
all stand unvalued beside all the material that you used.
So, what do you do when you find a liar in disguise?

24. Adult friendships

Adulting is hard
Adult friendships are harder.
You put your trust in someone new
Only to end up pretending to share a laugh or two.
You try hard to fit yourselves in.
But school and college friends are hard to forget like they were
your next to kin.
Adulting is hard.
Adult friendships are harder.
You can't share what's in your heart.
All you will get are judgmental eyes and a fake feeling of
warmth.
You still turn up to your old friends when you need an honest
review,
to shed long tears, and to share madness that's going through your
heart.
And not to forget, faking a smile,
and bitching behind your back is the new norm.
Because adulting is hard.
Adult friendships are harder.

25. Love and poetry

Dare not to fall in love with a girl who finds her existence into
poetries—
and worst of all, if she writes one.
She'll turn the ordinary into verse,
and you'll become nothing more than a fleeting muse.
She'll strip your heart bare,
then present it to the world,
claiming it as her own.
She'll make you feel like you're the only star in her sky,
only to turn away,
if another spark of artistry captures her imagination.
Beware of her if she writes without pause,
but fear her even more,
if she suddenly stops.
There's a tempest within her,
a flood she carries every single day.
She writes because her thoughts won't let her rest.
She writes because she's lost in a labyrinth of her own making.
She writes because words are her way of painting the world
onto paper.
Falling for her means drowning in her verses,
caught between the lines of her unfinished stories.

26. Unbecoming

Perhaps it's time to take that step.
Perhaps this night is meant for staying awake,
to master the art of unlearning one day,
and rediscovering the self by unbecoming along the way.
For years, I followed what was taught, but now,
it's time to let those lessons drift away.

I am ready to step into that phase,
with no intention of ever turning back.
Carrying the wisdom I've gathered through the years,
it's time to release the thought that
these moments were never truly what I ought to seek.

The art of letting go of the wrong people along the way,
Embracing self-love is all I wish to feel and convey.

Today, I long to master the art of unbecoming, this very moment,
this very day.

27. Crown

Let them think bad of you.
Let them stay mad at you.
You are not obliged to exist for the one.
You are not a kind who owes something to someone.
Once upon a time, a little girl stood up and straightened her
crown.

She waited for no one to come on a white horse and take her by
hand.
These were the stories she heard when she was young and carried
some wounds.
She carried all her pain on her sleeves.
And stood by her words when no one else did.
Once upon a time, a young woman stood up and straightened
her crown.

She knows her past was painful, and the future is yet to come.
So, she lives in the moment and hardly cares what others think.
She fell in love with a man and expressed her desire,
only to hear people say she has lost her mind,
and look at what she wishes to acquire.
And then, once again,
a queen stood up for herself and straightened her crown.

28. My Mother

Now that I think of my mother, I wonder how she must have felt.

Married at just 19, she had no close friends to confide in, no one to share her struggles with.

Her solace lay in letters, fragile lifelines to a world beyond her own.

While I called her instantly with a phone in hand, she relied on the slow rhythm of ink and paper to stay connected.

She sacrificed so much to make us who we are today.

Every decision she made, every hardship she endured, was for us.

We often talk about breaking cycles, about raising our children differently, but she too was breaking barriers in her own way.

Every day brought new challenges, and every moment demanded her resilience.

Now that I think of my mother, I see her not just as the woman who raised us but as a young girl who once had dreams of her own.

Dreams she quietly set aside, not because they mattered less, but because she chose to make ours possible.

She was, and is, remarkable in ways we are only beginning to understand.

29. Overrated

Happiness is so overrated
How can one stay happy all the time?
What's the purpose of sadness,
when happiness is what you always shrine?
There's no appreciation for dawn's first light,
if there's no existence of dark and dreading night.

Love is so overrated
How can one stay in love all the time?
The spark begins to fade once you start reading between the lines.
Eternal is just a word, a promise made is passion;
reality is what hits when you actually consign.

Like a fool, you keep chasing for both,
when all you need is to be in the present
and let life take its time and see its growth.
Permanence of something loses its beauty,
let the bittersweet essence of all the emotions shine equally.
This is how our lives are ever designed.

30. My Story Isn't Over Yet;

Because my story isn't over yet;
Once carefree and happy,
the girl I used to be no longer exists;
The tattoos on my arm speak another story of what it means;
Never have I ever thought of choosing the path that I still regret;
So just like that, my story isn't over yet;
Nights through the night, my thoughts kept me awake;
just to remind me of my worth, which isn't what I expected;
Thick through thin, I promised myself and,
wondered how could someone just choose to not exist and feel
worthless;
until and unless my steps dragged me in there,
and made me break the promise I made myself one day;

So just like that, my story isn't over yet;
When my fellow members once asked me to tell them the tale
behind it;
all ashamed I kept quiet and changed the topic just like that;
I will, I vow, that one day I will gather the courage to speak it
all;
and unburden my heart to become the person I was once with
the possibility to carry the truth;
So, until then, if you could read between the lines,
and promise to not judge me after knowing the fact,
then I would reveal you;
that just like that, my story isn't over yet;

31. Broken souls

Broken souls, sad and despised.
Let me heal them, I told my friends.
They warned me against the consequences and told me,
It will leave you with trust issues once again.
Broken souls with the remains of the past.
Let me try to erase them, I told my friends.
They warned me not to repeat that mistake,
as broken are the souls you always attract.
Broken souls looking for love.
Let me love them, I told my friends.
They told me, empathy is your enemy,
Don't let it win again and again.
Healed souls, who were once broken, caused me pain.
And like my friends said,
they left me with all the scars that I took away from them.

32. Melusina! The folklore of a beautiful mermaid

Broken promises are nothing new.
Not now, not then, but it has existed for centuries since we knew.
Standing by the river Alzette.
I heard about beautiful Melusina.
And the king who fell in love with her.
He made her a promise in a loving way.
But the civic had their other say.
They made him break the promise that he made to his love.
Never enter her chamber on a forbidden day.
So, that was the last time he saw her or had any other say.
She jumped into the Well.
Only to never return.
Oh, Melusina! You beauty,
why sacrifice yourself for someone,
who loved you but refused to keep the promise he made to you
one day?

33. Cursed

I walked through the deep tunnel,
and felt a bit scared.
Little did I know,
how life would be,
when there's no light out there.
At the end of the tunnel,
I found a high cliff.
With nothing beneath,
but only a dry ditch,
getting deeper and deeper when I tried to look through it.
I was standing on the edge,
Thinking how things would be
If I don't exist.

I have a friend; he is standing next to me
They say he doesn't exist
I am going through what they call a psychosis
There's a hush-hush sound
People ask me to keep quiet and not talk about it
Delusional thoughts are not welcome here, they say
But what do I do if I go through it every day
Standing on the edge.
I see no purpose to live
Depression is funny,
It tickles me every now and then.
But why do I cry with this tickling?
Why does it hurt me every time it comes near me?
I will jump and get this story over with,
Standing on the edge at the end of the tunnel,
I thought of this and saw my life ending under it.
(Say NO to TABOO over MENTAL HEALTH)

34. Men don't cry

And then they said, "Men don't cry".
You are strong and muscular, so don't be whiny.
Be a man because men don't cry.
You want to scream, you want to talk,
but somehow those spaces are reserved for a special lot,
because one day and every day they said, "Men don't cry".
You are in pain, and in an excruciating pain,
you had a heartbreak because you loved.
You hide your emotions because, once they say, "Men don't cry".

You lost someone you dearly loved,
you cry from the inside and hide your face,
because everyone else said, "Men don't cry".
You see no other way to find any peace with your pain,
so you put a smile on your face and with a thought of leaving
this world,
you remembered every word they said, "Men don't cry".
So STOP right there,
before you go any further with these thoughts of yours and others.
Unhide the little boy that you hide inside your little heart.
Because it's okay to not be okay.
because I stand by you and others do too.
Cry and cry until the time you find peace within yourself,
and let all your pain pass through the process.
Because these old rudimentary thoughts need to lose their path.
And let us make this very normal to one and all that men do cry.
Be it tears of joy or be it sorrow, "Men do cry".

35. Let you go

I have to let you go.
I have to LET ME let you go.
Deep conversations that we had once,
I have to let that all go.
Not because I want to forget you someday
but to let you enclose in my heart to never talk about you
anymore one day.
It's hard.
I know.
But I have to let me do that.
My heart craves too much of your attention,
but I know what it lacks is the right direction.
I convinced myself that somehow I didn't want to be part of this
race anymore.
I don't want to be on the list of your interests or even some more.
My heart feels lighter,
when I think of loving myself in the first place.
So, I have to let you go.
And I have to LET ME let you go.

36. Trust issues

You have been through a lot.
Your heart doesn't allow you to take another shot
No wonder why you fake that laugh
Either with highs or lows on your listed graph.

Because trusting someone comes at its own cost.

You gave yourself piece by piece
Thinking that things would never cease
Once, twice, thrice, and then endless times, you wished for luck.
and extended your wings to fly real high only to end up way
down and then being stuck.

Still, you get up with the same spirit you had before.
But this time, with a different personification and more.
Carrying with you all the insecurities and the trust issues you
gathered in a while all alone.

Because trusting someone comes at its own cost.

37. Story

How do I start this story anew?
From happiness to numbness, or leave it as history too?
Constantly worried about the unknown fears,
Raging heart, shaky hands, eyes brimming with tears.
My heart feels like it might burst from my chest,
And you will see me struggling, trying to find my nest.
They say their words didn't hurt, it came out of the blue,
But they don't see the scars, the pain that I knew.
I was once a cheerful girl, so full of light,
Whose only mistake was to love with all her might.
Caught in a whirl, a tempest of emotion,
drowning in a sea of unspoken devotion.

38. War and peace

If only men were selfish enough to choose not to go to wars

How the world would be?

Maybe more peaceful.

Maybe more chaos.

Men choose war to make themselves feel superior.

Women choose war to free themselves from all the barriers.

No one's greater than the other.

No one could survive without the other.

Let there be a world where we choose not war but peace.

Let us beat each other in exploring what lies beyond this.

When I look at the dark, beautiful sky, all our lives seem

meaningless.

All our wishes feel like a sham.

Then why choose war?

Let a world exist where men choose selfishness and do not go to

wars.

39. Overwhelmed

Overwhelmed by the situations,
I don't trouble people anymore.
Quietly, I just get lost in the woods,
Where no one traces me anymore.
Overwhelmed by the situations,
Tears don't drop like before.
Silently, I sit in peace,
And think about how far I have come near ashore.
Once during this time, just once,
fall in love with your pain.
You would understand that all that you went through,
was a process of healing and gain.

40. Before they leave

So many things left said-unsaid.
A last phone call, a last goodbye, tears still flowing -
one day, it would stop. So speak today.
Tell them what they mean to you.
Let them feel your words ring true.
Little do they know how special they are.
The smile they spread, the words they mean, their joyful eyes -
isn't it something worth telling them, how they made you feel?
Something inevitable, something true.
Yet we cling, afraid of that final adieu.
Time moves forward, yet hearts resist,
holding on to the moments we will one day miss.

41. The chaos inside me!

A loud crash echoes in my mind, heavy and relentless.
My heart pounds—slow yet urgent, as if trapped in a storm.
But why does the world seem untouched?
People walk past, laughing, unaware of the chaos inside me.
How can everything be so normal when my thoughts are
unravelling?
Every time I think of you, my mind feels like it's about to break.
Slowly, I pulled myself together,
forcing myself to meet people's eyes when they greeted me.
But now, when I try to hide my pain, their gaze feels sharp,
almost knowing.
Their silence makes me uneasy—what if they know?
What if they ask?
How will I hide these tears waiting to spill over?

42. Wait

Pages still folded.
A rose hidden somewhere in between,
papers crumbled around,
and an overflowing bin.

He went through her pictures every now and then,
only to regret the confession that he never dared to pen.
He was a writer,
She was his hidden muse.
They lived together,
but were always confused.

Looking outside the window,
He spoke of his heart one day.
Only to realise she was listening to something odd that day.
Before he could talk of something more,
She took a pill and went to sleep.

That was the last time he saw her
just to discover she would never rise again.
Now that she is no longer here,
He still waits for her by the door,
but no one could see his pain anymore.

And then there on day, the new tenants entered the gate.
It's cold, dark, and eerie — the people said,
The ventilation is excellent — that is what the broker explained.
While he quietly sits in a corner with a pen in his hand,
and waits for her muse to return from her sleep one day.

43. Romantic Love

Someone once asked me, "Why don't you believe in romantic love?"

Well, listen—

First of all, love, to me, is just a cocktail of hormones,

and a symphony of brain chemicals doing their thing.

But that doesn't mean I don't crave something real.

I may come off as stubborn,

but the truth is—I'm built for a softer kind of love.

The kind where my overthinking isn't dismissed,

Where the joy I find in a cup of hot coffee turned cold isn't ridiculed.

The kind of love that doesn't expect me to be strong all the time,

That gives me space to be soft, to be seen, to just be.
The kind where I can laugh till my stomach hurts,
And cry till my mascara runs—without feeling the need to
apologize for the mess.
The kind that doesn't compete with my love for food,
That doesn't make me feel like I have to carry everything
alone—
Because they're right there, carrying it with me.
*So maybe, if I ever stumble upon *that* kind of love,*
I'll stop over-analyzing the science of it all,
And for once—
Let myself feel it, fully, irrationally, beautifully.

44. Empty!

I stared at a piece of paper.
With pen in my hand,
and a deep desire to write something finer.
With utter excitement, I bent to start with an intriguing topic.
Suddenly, I felt lost.
And all I did was continuously gawk,
waiting for words to just fall out from my brain.
After a lot of struggling days, the paper remained as it is,
just like my feelings per se - EMPTY!

Thankyou For Reading Me!

If a single line stays with you, or if something here quietly resonates, then this space has already served its purpose. Thank you for taking a moment to wander through these words. Whenever you feel like returning, these poems will be here, waiting — ready to speak when you're ready to listen.

www.ingramcontent.com/pod-product-compliance
Lightning Source LLC
Chambersburg PA
CBHW020509160726
47991CB00007B/2871